IOWA'S
LOST SUMMER

The Flood of 1993

IOWA'S LOST SUMMER

The Flood of 1993

Edited and designed by Michael Wegner, Lyle Boone and Tim Cochran
Photographs by The Des Moines Register *staff*

Iowa State University Press and Des Moines Register and Tribune Company

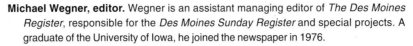

Michael Wegner, editor. Wegner is an assistant managing editor of *The Des Moines Register*, responsible for the *Des Moines Sunday Register* and special projects. A graduate of the University of Iowa, he joined the newspaper in 1976.

Lyle Boone, designer. Boone is an assistant managing editor of *The Des Moines Register,* responsible for design, photography and graphics. He has bachelor's and master's degrees from Drake University and has worked at the newspaper since 1967.

Tim Cochran, photo editor. Cochran is photo director of *The Des Moines Register.* He joined the newspaper in 1993 from *The Virginian Pilot.* A graduate of the University of Missouri, he also has worked for newspapers in Missouri, West Virginia and Iowa.

Cover photograph by David Peterson; back cover photograph by Bill Neibergall

———◆———

© 1993 Des Moines Register and Tribune Company, Des Moines, Iowa 50309
All rights reserved

Co-published by Iowa State University Press, Ames, Iowa 50014, and the Des Moines Register and Tribune Company, Des Moines, Iowa 50309

Printed by ACME Printing Co., Inc., Des Moines/Ames, Iowa, 50314, on acid-free, recycled paper.

No part of this book may be reproduced in any form or by any electronic or mechanical means, including information storage and retrieval systems, without written permission from the publishers, except for brief passages quoted in a review.

First edition, 1993
Second printing, 1993
Third printing, 1993

Library of Congress Cataloging-in-Publication Data

Des Moines Register.
Iowa's Lost Summer: The Flood of 1993. Book design and editing by Michael Wegner, Lyle Boone and Tim Cochran; photographs by The Des Moines Register staff.

p. cm.
ISBN 0-8138-1809-5

1. Floods — Iowa — Pictorial works. 2. Floods — Des Moines River Valley (Minn. and Iowa) — Pictorial works. 3. Floods — Mississippi River Valley — Pictorial works. 4. Iowa — Pictorial works. 5. Des Moines River Valley (Minn. and Iowa) — Pictorial works. 6. Mississippi River Valley — Pictorial works. I. Wegner, Michael. II. Boone, Lyle. III. Cochran, Tim. IV. Iowa State University Press. V. Title.

F622.D47 1993
977.7'033 — dc20

93-30245
CIP

This book is dedicated to the memory of
Spc. Steven M. West, 30, a National Guard soldier from
Ogden, Iowa, who was electrocuted July 16, 1993, while on duty in
Des Moines. He was erecting an antenna to allow
communications with water trucks when the antenna
touched a high-power line.

◆

And to the friends and families of April Dedrick, 22, and
Sayna Lee Stewart, 19, both of Vinton; Vernon Neiderhiser, 70, of Ely;
Donald Sealine, 64, and his wife, Bernadine, 67, of rural Dexter; and
Kenneth W. Tille, 43, of Knoxville. All died in
flood-related traffic accidents.

◆

And to the people of Iowa, who not only endured adversity, but
who also triumphed.

Contents

Marcial Castillo, 3, was one of the many Des Moines residents who had to stand in line for water when the Des Moines Water Works flooded on July 11. With Marcial is Jose Rojas, 8.

KAREN MITCHELL

Foreword

Gov. Terry Branstad with President Clinton and Iowa Army National Guard Col. Roger Schultz.

JEFFREY Z. CARNEY

A dversity is the true test of character. Iowans met the challenge of the flood of 1993 with courage, hard work and a determination to overcome the worst natural disaster in our state's history and to help each other move ahead.

Neighbors are helping neighbors. People who suffered losses are helping others who are still in the fight. The outpouring of volunteers and contributions is bolstering our efforts to save lives, protect property, clean up the mess and restore life to normal.

Iowans are grateful for the support that is pouring in from throughout the nation. That battle is not over. I am proud of the way Iowans have shown their willingness to help each other win this battle. We are determined to help the various government agencies, volunteers and contributors to deliver assistance as fast as possible to the people who need it.

Iowans are united in our indomitable spirit to succeed, despite adversity.

— Governor Terry E. Branstad
August 10, 1993

These cartoons by Des Moines Register cartoonist Brian Duffy appeared in the newspaper on July 21 and July 23, 1993 .

Preface

The Story of Iowa's Lost Summer

◆

Of all the ironies of the summer of '93, one in particular stands out here at *The Des Moines Register*: One of the paper's principal reporting projects for this summer was to have been an in-depth look at the Des Moines River.

We called it "Exploring the Des Moines River." It began on Sunday, May 30.

It ended on Sunday, May 30.

No sooner had *Register* reporters begun their trip down the Des Moines than it became unnavigable because of the high waters. Indeed, rampaging rivers everywhere had begun taking over life in Iowa.

The flood swept across the state, from the Mississippi to the Missouri. Along with the seemingly endless rain, the flood's impact was felt in every county, devastating crops, ruining homes and businesses, and making a distant memory of the summertime activities that Iowans so enjoy.

This book is the story of that lost summer. It is river reporting, all right, but reporting of a very different sort than planned.

◆

For a century and more, *The Register* has chronicled life in Iowa, a state with an unusual sense of cohesion. In line with

JULY 10, 1993

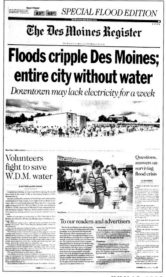

JULY 12, 1993

that tradition, throughout the late spring and early summer our staff was neck-deep into covering the developing flood story.

Hundreds of stories were written. Reporters slept on cots and ate Red Cross dinners as we followed the fates of the state's eastern border, pounded day after day by the Mississippi.

By the weekend of July 10 and 11, the newsroom was tight as a drum, overworked and cranky, and editors were pondering how to relieve the pressure.

That's when the flood struck Des Moines.

In the early morning hours of Sunday, July 11, Iowa's flood of '93 grabbed the state's largest city by the throat.

The entire city was knocked out. Power was widely interrupted. Homes and businesses were inundated, traffic flow cut off. A quarter of a million people were to go 19 days without drinking water.

It was one more escalation in a summer when it seemed as if the flood just wouldn't let go. The rains pounded with biblical intensity. The next record downpour, the next river crest, the next flash flood, seemed always imminent.

Like other Iowans, *The Register* relied on the kindness of neighbors for its survival. The newspaper of Monday, July 12, was an eight-page edition distributed in the metropolitan area only. It was reported from an emergency newsroom at the University Park Holiday Inn in West Des Moines and assembled in the newsroom of the *Indianola Record-Herald*. The page negatives were flown to Iowa City where it was printed on *Press-Citizen* presses.

For the next two weeks, lack of water kept *The Register* from printing at its downtown site. Papers were printed at the *Wall Street Journal's* plant in West Des Moines, and in Iowa City.

The newspaper staff worked in 90-degree-plus temperatures, then went home to waterless homes and families. In every department, employees labored to overcome lack of power, lack of water, mud, bridges out, cities swamped and more, to get the paper out and across the state.

It was the sort of thing Iowans everywhere were experiencing, the sort of thing that brought people together and made them feel powerful appreciation for one another.

Iowa has always seemed a special place to live and to do newspapering, a state with

JULY 23, 1993

JULY 24, 1993

an unusually strong sense of community. Never has that sense been more sorely tested, or shown itself stronger, than in the flood of '93.

The flood, of course, struck much of the Midwest. Other states have their own stories of tragedy and bravery.

But this is Iowa's story. It is the faces of Iowans, and the emotions they felt — anguish, loss, astonishment at the generous help offered — that are reflected in these pages.

And this, appropriately, is an Iowa book, published with the Iowa State University Press and printed by Acme Printing Company, a Des Moines company that was flooded and out of business for two weeks.

This book is the culmination of the most extraordinary company-wide effort ever by *The Register's* 1,127 employees and more than 4,000 carriers.

It is published in recognition of all Iowans, all over the state, who pulled together to overcome the greatest natural disaster in Iowa's history.

— *Geneva Overholser*
Editor, The Des Moines Register

IOWA'S
LOST SUMMER

The Flood of 1993

FLOODING ALONG IOWA RIVERS

HERE'S A look at flood levels and the peak flood levels of Iowa's major rivers and creeks.

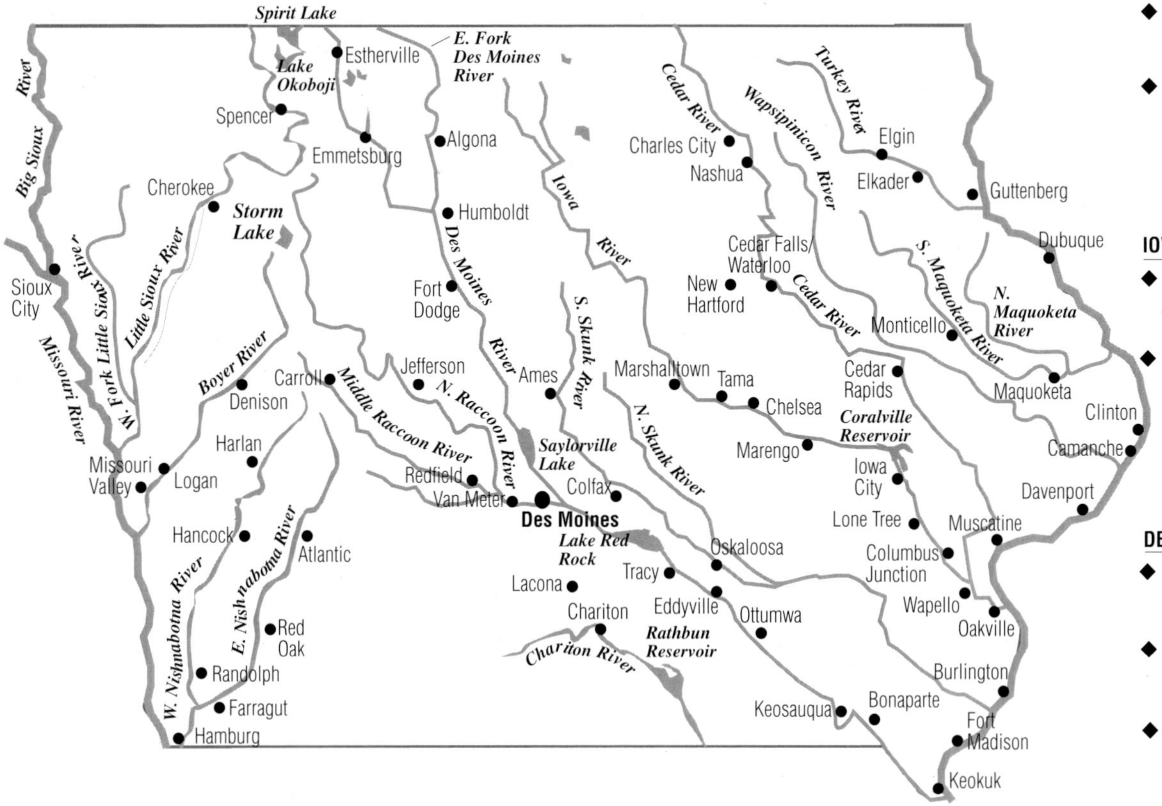

Map labels (rivers, lakes, cities):

Spirit Lake, E. Fork Des Moines River, Estherville, Lake Okoboji, Spencer, Emmetsburg, Algona, Cherokee, Storm Lake, Humboldt, Fort Dodge, Des Moines River, Jefferson, N. Raccoon River, Ames, Carroll, Boyer River, Denison, Middle Raccoon River, Harlan, Saylorville Lake, Redfield, Van Meter, Colfax, Des Moines, Lake Red Rock, Lacona, Chariton, Rathbun Reservoir, Chariton River, Eddyville, Tracy, Oskaloosa, Ottumwa, Keosauqua, Bonaparte, Fort Madison, Keokuk

Big Sioux River, Sioux City, Missouri River, W. Fork Little Sioux River, Little Sioux River, Missouri Valley, Logan, Hancock, Atlantic, W. Nishnabotna River, E. Nishnabotna River, Red Oak, Randolph, Farragut, Hamburg

Iowa River, S. Skunk River, N. Skunk River, Charles City, Nashua, Cedar River, Wapsipinicon River, Turkey River, Elgin, Elkader, Guttenberg, Dubuque, Cedar Falls/Waterloo, New Hartford, Cedar River, Marshalltown, Tama, Chelsea, Marengo, Cedar Rapids, Coralville Reservoir, Iowa City, Lone Tree, S. Maquoketa River, N. Maquoketa River, Monticello, Maquoketa, Clinton, Camanche, Davenport, Muscatine, Columbus Junction, Wapello, Oakville, Burlington

MISSISSIPPI RIVER

◆ **Camanche**
Flood stage: **16**
Peak July 8: **22.96**

◆ **Davenport**
Flood stage: **15**
Peak July 9: **22.65**

◆ **Muscatine**
Flood stage: **16**
Peak July 9: **25.61**

◆ **Burlington**
Flood stage: **15**
Peak July 10: **24.96**

◆ **Keokuk**
Flood stage: **16**
Peak July 10: **27.15**

IOWA RIVER

◆ **Iowa City**
Flood stage: **22**
Peak Aug. 10: **28.52**

◆ **Marengo**
Flood stage: **14**
Peak July 19: **20.27**

◆ **Marshalltown**
Flood stage: **13**
Peak July10: **20.55**

◆ **Wapello**
Flood stage: **20**
Peak July 7: **29.53**

◆ **Near Lone Tree**
Flood stage: **15**
Peak July 7: **22.94**

DES MOINES RIVER

◆ **Estherville**
Flood stage: **7**
Peak July 10: **15.21**

◆ **Near Tracy**
Flood stage: **14**
Peak July 12: **24.16**

◆ **Near Ottumwa**
Flood stage: **10**
Peak July 12: **22.13**

◆ **Near Saylorville**
Flood stage: **23**
Peak July 11: **24.12**

◆ **S.E. 14th Street (DM)**
Flood stage: **23**
Peak July 11: **34.29**

◆ **Keosauqua**
Flood stage: **25**
Peak July 13: **32.66**

FIGURES EXPRESSED IN FEET

NISHNABOTNA RIVER

◆ **Above Hamburg**
Flood stage: **16**
Peak July 23: **30.52**

WEST NISHNABOTNA RIVER

◆ **At Hancock**
Flood stage: **19**
Peak July 10: **23.53**

SOUTH SKUNK RIVER

◆ **Below Squaw Creek near Ames**
Flood stage: **7**
Peak July 9: **25.53**

◆ **At Colfax**
Flood stage: **17**
Peak July 10: **19.40**

◆ **Near Oskaloosa**
Flood stage: **15**
Peak July 15: **25.16**

SQUAW CREEK

◆ **Ames**
Flood stage: **7**
Peak July 9: **18.54**

CHARITON RIVER

◆ **Chariton**
Flood stage: **15**
Peak July 6: **22.37**

RACCOON RIVER

◆ **Van Meter**
Flood stage: **13**
Peak July 10: **25.83**

SOUTH RACCOON RIVER

◆ **Redfield**
Flood stage: **14**
Peak July 10: **27.09**

SOURCES: U.S. Army Corps of Engineers, National Weather Service

Overview

A Season of Misery

◆

"When that river is in its banks it's a beautiful thing to see. This is the dark side."

— **Helen Joiner,** co-owner of a Davenport pawn shop, commenting on the record floods of 1993

"Tornadoes are easy. They're gone and done with. Floods are tougher."

— **Carol Grant,** Red Cross official in Des Moines

The first hints of trouble came from an outpost in northeast Iowa on Wednesday, March 31.

Record water levels on a Cedar River tributary — churned by heavy rains and melting snow — inundated, then isolated, New Hartford. Downstream and on other rivers, Cedar Falls, Waterloo, Tama, Marshalltown, Chelsea and other communities braced for possible record flooding.

No one who awoke on April 1 to read the dispatch from New Hartford could have known it foretold the calamity that lay ahead.

Iowa was about to endure a season of misery unlike any other.

There was special suffering to be sure: the 376 residents of Chelsea who could be forgiven for losing count of the times they had to evacuate their homes; the quarter-million parched residents of the Des Moines area who went 19 days without drinking water after flooding knocked out the water-treatment plant; the farmers and small-business owners who lost everything.

But it was the egalitarian nature of the floods of 1993 that Iowans long will remember. All quarters of the state suffered.

By the time the rivers quit raging, seven people were dead; more

Thousands of Iowans suffered from the flooding. Russ Vourlet of West Des Moines lost valuable plumbing tools to the rampaging Raccoon River.

DOUG WELLS

than 21,000 houses, apartments and mobile homes were destroyed or damaged; crop losses were pegged at $1 billion and rising as farmers stared at an uncertain harvest, and total damage was conservatively estimated at $2.7 billion.

"We've been hit by the worst natural disaster in our state's history," Gov. Terry Branstad said during an interview in late July on Iowa Public Television.

President Bill Clinton, on the second of two inspection visits to Iowa within a two-week period in early July, toured Des Moines by helicopter and proclaimed, "I have never seen anything on this scale before....

"It was awful."

Floods are indeed tougher.

◆

Old-timers could recall other terrible Iowa floods. Hamburg remembers 1952, when a Missouri River levee broke, sending a wall of water crashing down on the city. Des Moines River historians still talk about 1947. In Davenport and points south, 1965 and 1973 were the worst. Until the summer of 1993.

In 1993, all of Iowa's rivers seemed angry. The Mississippi and Missouri. The Des Moines and Raccoon. The Nishnabotna and Wapsipinicon. The Iowa and Skunk. The Little Sioux and Cedar. The Boyer and Turkey. A lot of creeks and streams weren't too pleased, either.

An overly simple explanation of complex weather patterns might lay the blame for Iowa's rotten 1993 weather on the jet stream, the river of westerly winds in the upper atmosphere. Typically, the jet stream shifts northward into Canada during the summer, allowing weather systems — including the ones causing rain — to pass through the state.

In the summer of '93, the jet stream stalled over Iowa and the Midwest like a lid on a mason jar. A high-pressure system over the eastern part of the country pumped moisture-laden air from the Gulf of Mexico north. That air bumped into the jet stream parked over Iowa and dumped its moisture on the spot.

Rainfall amounts were staggering.

Through the middle of August, Iowa had 12 consecutive weeks of above-normal rainfall. The average state rainfall for July was more than 10 inches, the highest July total in 121 years of state record keeping.

"If you're writing a disaster script, you probably wouldn't write statistics as ridiculous as what happened," said Harry Hillaker, the state climatologist. "It would seem too incredible."

In the Des Moines River valley, especially from Estherville to Fort Dodge, the rains seemed never to end between April and June. Just when floodwaters would start to recede from fields and roads, it would rain again.

The nearby Iowa Great Lakes at Okoboji were as much as 4 feet above normal. With water that high, county officials were working to save inundated homes by lowering the lakes before they began their annual freeze.

Later, central and southern Iowans would share those problems. Water from northern Iowa flowed into two rapidly filling reservoirs — Saylorville, just north of Des Moines, and Red Rock, just south of the capital — setting the stage for bigger trouble later.

In June and early July, continuing heavy rains roiled many Iowa rivers, causing normally placid streams to mutiny.

The Mississippi River set high-water records at several spots along the Iowa border.

The Boyer River at Logan rose 15.7 feet in 24 hours on July 9. That same day, the Nishnabotna at Hamburg rose 6.85 feet, while the Raccoon at Van Meter rose 6.33 feet, all in a few hours.

In Ames, both the Skunk River and Squaw Creek jumped their banks. On the Iowa State University campus, Hilton Coliseum filled with 14 feet of water — up to the first row of

parquet-level seats. University buildings sustained an estimated $7.7 million in damage.

The battle against rising rivers also extracted an emotional toll.

"Every day I get up and say, 'God please, no more. We've had enough,'" said Nancy Breuklander of Ottumwa.

◆

When the Iowa floods of 1993 recede to a memory, central Iowans will be left with some of the wildest stories to tell grandchildren.

Those stories will begin with the 10 inches of rain that fell north and west of Des Moines on Thursday, July 8. Fueled by all that water, the Raccoon and Des Moines rivers took dead aim on Iowa's population center.

In West Des Moines on July 10, a sandbag wall built by hundreds of volunteers and National Guard troops was simply no match for a river that was rising nearly one foot every hour.

Floodwaters from the Raccoon swept under the sandbags, washed out railroad tracks along Railroad Avenue and spilled into the Valley Junction area, swamping businesses and forcing the evacuation of 5,000 residents there and in Des Moines.

The worst was yet to come.

As the river pushed south and east into Des Moines, it overran levees protecting the Des

Moines Water Works. Having lost a battle they never dreamed they'd have to fight, waterworks officials surrendered to prevent additional damage.

At 3:02 a.m. Sunday, July 11, Gary Benjamin, the director of water production, turned off the motors that drove the giant pumps. "I had this sick feeling in my stomach," Benjamin said. "I hit that last switch and we were out of business. The whole city was out of business."

The result: A city of a quarter-million people was without running water; its fire hydrants empty; its hospitals crippled; its people the victims of one of the greatest threats to public safety and health imaginable.

Most downtown businesses closed for up to two weeks, idling thousands of workers.

The 19 days the city went without drinking water were agonizing ones. As waterworks officials scrambled to restore water, there were unfortunate, and tragic, incidents.

Some thugs vandalized Des Moines' Sec Taylor Stadium. Several stranded homes were burglarized. Con artists surfaced. There were reports of price gouging on some out-of-town portable toilet rentals. And some residents and businesses were caught snitching water before they were authorized to do so.

Spc. Steven M. West, 30, of Ogden, one of the 4,200 National Guard soldiers who served Iowa heroically during the flooding, died

A wedding album belonging to David and Joyce Wright of Des Moines lies discarded because of water damage from the flood that ravaged their neighborhood.

DAVID PETERSON

when the communications antenna he was erecting touched a high-power line.

But there is good news in this story, and this is where it begins.

There were more examples of people helping people than could be told in a book 10 times this size.

Hurricane-battered Floridians, who had been assisted a year earlier by Iowans, traveled to the Midwest with water and mops to repay the favor. Volunteers from Minnesota, Wisconsin, Colorado, Pennsylvania and elsewhere showed up eager to work. Breweries filled beer cans with water and shipped them to Des Moines. Cedar Rapids police lent their Des Moines colleagues a helicopter so they could patrol flooded areas.

And throughout it all, there were stories that would not surprise long-time Iowans.

One came in the form of a complaint from federal disaster-relief officials that proud Iowans were hesitating to sign up for flood aid.

"They are all taxpayers. If they could just look at this as their tax dollars being returned to them," said Jane Vukonich of the Federal Emergency Management Agency, who speculated that some residents perceived the money as some sort of welfare program.

◆

Even as summer drew to a close, the flooding refused to abate.

Water flowed over the spillway at the Rathbun Dam near Centerville for the first time ever, prompting the rural water association that serves much of southern Iowa to build an emergency water line.

In the Iowa City-Coralville area, flooding on Clear Creek on August 12 added to more than a month's worth of problems for beleaguered residents and businesses. University officials had to scramble to find replacement classrooms and dorm rooms before classes resumed August 23.

In the third week of August, the Cedar River took aim at Charles City, Nashua, Waverly, Cedar Falls and Waterloo.

And just days before the State Fair began on August 19, Ames was flooded for the third time, Tama for the fourth, and tiny Chelsea for the fifth.

Jerry Veit of Chelsea, whose house had just been cleaned and disinfected after sustaining $14,000 in damages from earlier flooding, found himself staring wearily at another soggy mess.

"We just hope this is the last one," he said.

— *Michael Wegner*
August 20, 1993

Sec Taylor Stadium flooded July 11. The stadium is home to the Iowa Cubs professional baseball team.

BOB NANDELL

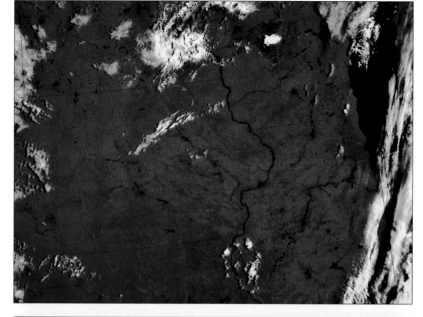

Satellite photographs from about 500 miles show what rain did to Iowa's landscape in July 1992 (top), versus July 1993. The white tones represent clouds, the green is healthy vegetation and the dark tones show water or saturated soils. The images were processed by the United States Geological Survey's EROS Data Center in Sioux Falls, S.D.

EROS DATA CENTER

Uwe Richardson and his son, Melvin, 8, sit atop some of their equipment being stored at the farm of relatives near Sidney. Richardson expected to salvage only 10 percent of his corn crop and even less of his soybeans.

TERESA HURTEAU

Iowa crop losses were pegged at $1 billion early in the summer. Crop specialists said an early frost would send losses higher. This submerged soybean field is near Hamburg.

BILL NEIBERGALL

State workers line up to use the portable toilets in the Statehouse parking lot the day after Des Moines lost its water. An estimated 6,000 state workers at the Capitol complex worked throughout the flood crisis.

PAUL HISCOCKS

A two-story frame house across the Iowa River from Wapello was knocked off its foundation after a levee broke in early July. Though no one was living in the house, it contained furniture and clothing belonging to the daughter of owner Larry Lihs of Wapello.

HARRY BAUMERT

Ruth Wood, who lost many of her belongings when her east-side Des Moines home flooded, is comforted by her daughter, Patty Savage, and by friend Ralph Prather. At right, Patty Savage salvages pictures of Jesus and of her mother. The pictures were two of the items that survived 5 feet of floodwater.

DAVID PETERSON

Christina Hein, 24, weeps as she and President Clinton embrace during the president's July 14 visit to a water-distribution site at Des Moines' SouthRidge Mall. Hein told Clinton: "Mr. President, we need help." Clinton also toured Des Moines by helicopter and helped to fill sandbags near the Raccoon River.

JEFFREY Z. CARNEY

Harold and Ruby McCullough watch floodwater rise around their sandbag-surrounded house as a pump removes water from their basement in Buffalo July 1. Buffalo is just downstream from Davenport.

HARRY BAUMERT

The Mississippi River covered River Drive in downtown Davenport on June 29. The bridge to Arsenal Island and Lock and Dam 15 is at bottom. John O'Donnell Stadium and LeClaire Park are at upper left.

HARRY BAUMERT

Sandbaggers work furiously to build a levee on the Raccoon River in Van Meter July 10, when the river rose more rapidly than expected. Van Meter is just west of Des Moines.

A determined-looking volunteer, Terri Vaughan, passes sandbags during feverish efforts July 13 to reinforce the levee around the West Des Moines Water Works. The levee held, preserving the water supply for 30,000 West Des Moines residents.

JEFFREY Z. CARNEY

A front-end loader evacuates West Des Moines reserve police officer Butch Stuckert and his all-terrain vehicle moments after a levee began spilling floodwaters onto city streets July 10. Others, in background, evacuate Fifth Street in the Valley Junction area, a dry street only moments before.

JEFFREY Z. CARNEY

An Amish girl from Drakesville, who declined to give her name because of religious beliefs, helped with sandbagging efforts on a humid July day in Ottumwa.

JAY P. WAGNER

**National Guard troops shovel sand from the top of a truck at Railroad Avenue in West Des Moines
July 10, in what turned out to be a vain effort to shore up the levee.**

GARY FANDEL

Where the Hurting Began

◆

"When you have six floods in three years, don't tell me about disaster."

— **Ed Johnston**, Chelsea Mayor

A number of Iowa cities were damaged by flooding early. Others were flooded later in the summer. A few got clobbered on both ends.

Chelsea was among the latter.

This small Tama County town became one of Iowa's first flooding victims of 1993 in April, when residents evacuated the surging waters of the Iowa River and Otter Creek.

By August, Chelsea had flooded four more times and emergency measures had become a way of life for its 376 residents.

The town lost its drinking water in early July, and residents were still drinking bottled water in August.

"Even though we're small, we've got the same hurts as a large town," Mayor Johnston said, while making an appeal for aid to help save his town.

Iowans living along and near the Des Moines River also were among the victims of both spring and summer flooding.

In Emmetsburg, the Des Moines River was above flood stage four times in April and May alone.

A few miles north of Emmetsburg, there was so much rain at Okoboji and Spirit Lake that residents worried about irrevocable damage to the shoreline of one of Iowa's most popular vacation destinations.

Near Boone, the river submerged the popular Ledges State Park for much of the summer and inflicted its worst damage in 50 years.

Mark Steele straddles sandbags in front of his father's house in Orleans, near Spirit Lake.

DOUG WELLS

Downstream, the giant dams and reservoirs built by the Army Corps of Engineers were no match for the river. Whenever residents of Eddyville and Ottumwa looked upstream, all they could see were the surging waters of the Des Moines, barely slowed by passage through Saylorville and Red Rock reservoirs. Anxious residents grew weary from filling sandbags.

Low-lying sections of Ottumwa flooded in early July and stayed under water for more than a month, leaving more than 200 families homeless.

On July 12, Eddyville (pop. 1,116) finally abandoned an eight-day fight to protect its two-mile-long sandbag levee when the levee started to give way.

At the same time Eddyville was retreating, it was demonstrating why the river often wins the battles, but rarely the war.

Instead of giving up when the levee failed, Eddyville residents just changed tactics. Gilbert Gillogly, who retired as a school principal in southern California before moving to Eddyville to open a market, was one of the beneficiaries of the strategy.

"The highest point of my life came today," he said as the battle with the river was being lost. "I had planned to just close the store when the floods came, say 'bye bye' and take my losses. But I had 75 people show up to help me move out of here.

"These are wonderful people." ■

Agriculture Secretary Mike Espy, flanked by Gov. Terry Branstad and Sen. Tom Harkin, toured the flood-damaged farm of Dalen Miller in north-central Iowa near Dumont on June 30.

HARRY BAUMERT

Northern Iowa was especially hard hit by rain and flooding in early spring. This flooded farm field is near Emmetsburg, where the Des Moines River was above flood stage four times in April and May. Threatening skies appeared over this farm between Humboldt and Algona on June 14.

GARY FANDEL
BOB MODERSOHN

Boats were the only reliable form of transportation for many rural Iowans.
Here, some boats are beached on a gravel road southeast of Ottumwa.

BOB NANDELL

An unidentified water skier takes advantage of what used
to be a soybean field near Turin in western Iowa.

LOREN SAWYER

**Ronald Clemann of Keystone returned to his hometown of Chelsea on July 19
and spent nine hours helping flood victims get in and out of town. His father is
the assistant fire chief.**

JAMIE GERMANO

**Leonard Behounek of Chelsea gives an
appreciative wave with a jug of water
delivered for him and his wife.**

HARRY BAUMERT

A bulldozer driven by Terry McMullen reinforces a levee in Eddyville.

HARRY BAUMERT

This bank was one of the Eddyville businesses forced to close by the flooding Des Moines River.

JAY P. WAGNER

Joyce Van Galen, center, of Leighton, and Brenda Roberts, right, of rural Eddyville, work to save a levee in Eddyville on July 12.

HARRY BAUMERT

Joshua Dye bails water from his boat in Eldon. Dye was helping to evacuate residents when Chippewa Creek swamped the southeast Iowa town.

TERESA HURTEAU

A mobile home park in the Rabbit Run area on the southeast edge of Ottumwa was evacuated after being flooded on July 6.

DOUG WELLS

Dick Damm of Ottumwa surveys damage in the Rabbit Run area. Water was more than 12 feet high.

JAMIE GERMANO

Water from the Des Moines River was 18 inches high inside Ivan Mitchell's 19th-century building in downtown Bonaparte. Here, Mitchell, 70, cleans up after water receded.

HARRY BAUMERT

Life on the Mississippi

◆

*"One who knows the Mississippi will promptly aver — not aloud but
to himself — that 10,000 River Commissions, with the mines
of the world at their back, cannot tame that lawless stream,
cannot curb it or confine it, cannot say to it,
'Go here,' or 'Go there,' and make it obey . . . ."*

— **Mark Twain,** *Life on the Mississippi*

On July 2, just as the Mississippi River was expected to finally crest in Davenport, the *Quad-City Times* ran an enormous front-page headline: THIS IS IT!

A week later, the river was back, higher than ever.

It was like that all along the Mississippi River all summer long. A smart Iowan was one who kept a wary eye on the river.

The Mississippi first reached flood stage at Davenport on June 11. Almost two months later, the river was still above flood stage, although considerably below the devastating levels of early July, when the river crested 7 feet above flood stage at Davenport and 10 feet above flood stage at Burlington, both records.

"I'm not sure if a crest means anything," Davenport Mayor Pat Gibbs said the day before the record crest. "How many 'crests' have we had this week?"

When the Mississippi floods, it attracts national attention because the river has become a metaphor for an America that is powerful, fluid and ever-changing. Along the river in

**High water and closed locks on the Mississippi River
stalled barge traffic from late June until August.**

HARRY BAUMERT

Iowa, the river is more than a metaphor.

"We have barge terminals here. We have businesses that are here because of the river. We have a tourist trade that is directly tied to the river," said Mayor Gibbs, who just as easily could have been speaking for Iowa's other river cities.

For all that the river usually gives to these cities, this time it responded by leaving commerce along its banks in shambles.

About half of Keokuk's 2,500-person work force was idled when three of the town's biggest factories, all located by the river, were flooded.

Hundreds of people were temporarily out of work in the Fort Madison area when at least five large companies were paralyzed by the flood. Downtown Burlington sustained heavy damage.

The Santa Fe Railroad quit running due to water over the tracks.

Bridges in Keokuk and Fort Madison were closed, and traffic back-ups of an hour or more were common on the bridge in Burlington.

In Lee County, water stood anywhere from 2 feet to 20 feet deep over about three-quarters of the 17,000-acre area in Green Bay Bottoms after a dike broke there on July 11.

Three feet of water flowed over a road to the gate of the maximum-security prison at Fort Madison, and a temporary road also was flooded. Some 150 inmates were allowed outside the prison walls to help sandbagging efforts.

Barge traffic on the Mississippi was stopped June 25 when high water made commercial navigation impossible. Eventually, 11 of the 12 locks between Dubuque and Hannibal, Mo., would close until August.

The standstill idled 5,000 of the active fleet of 20,000 barges on the Mississippi and about 7 million tons of barge freight — mostly grain, coal and petroleum — valued at $1.6 billion.

By early August, signs of normalcy had returned along the river. Bridges were open. Most businesses were drying out. Debates about flood control were once again raging. And river-city Iowans seemed certain they would bounce back, even if they couldn't make the river obey. ■

**Bob Fitzgibbon
watches water being
pumped out of the
AAA Muffler Shop in
Davenport as the
Mississippi River
continued to rise on
July 4. The Fitzgib-
bon family kept nine
pumps going.**

HARRY BAUMERT

**Grant Prochaska, 5, of Ely, checks out a dead catfish near
Harrison Street and River Drive in Davenport.**

BILL NEIBERGALL

Minor-league baseball was a casualty of the flooding in Davenport. Floodwaters covered the field at John O'Donnell Stadium, home of the Class A River City Bandits.

HARRY BAUMERT

While helping relatives move, Christina Daufeldt, 15, Roger Gillespie, 17, and Carl Fetty, 22, had to wade through floodwaters in Davenport July 1.

BILL NEIBERGALL

Inmates from the Iowa State Penitentiary place sandbags around Fort Madison's riverfront pavilion on July 2.

HARRY BAUMERT

President Clinton is nearly upstaged by 9-year-old Joe Schneckloth in Eldridge July 4. Clinton met with farmers at the farm of Joe's parents, Don and Elaine Schneckloth.

BILL NEIBERGALL

President Clinton, dressed in blue jeans, green shirt and cowboy boots, discussed Mississippi River flooding with Gov. Terry Branstad and local officials on a Davenport bridge on July 4. Agriculture Secretary Mike Espy is at far right.

BILL NEIBERGALL

Though the basement of Brad Bowers' Pleasant Valley home was full of muddy Mississippi River water, the raised deck outside his back door was high and dry — a good place for a little fishing. He holds a stringer of catfish he caught from a lawn chair.

HARRY BAUMERT

Bob Carhoff, a Burlington city engineer, uses a temporary walkway to navigate the flooded parking lot at the city's Municipal Auditorium. At the flood's high point, more than 5 feet of water filled the building.

HARRY BAUMERT

Volunteer Ron Mace checks the pumps that were keeping
water out of the North Lee County Historical Society Building
in Fort Madison.

HARRY BAUMERT

Trees and homes rise out of Mississippi
River water covering Abel Island on the
north side of Guttenberg June 29.

HARRY BAUMERT

**John McCormick of Burlington stacks some of his household
possessions on tables after floodwaters entered his home.**

HARRY BAUMERT

"It's Just Water All Over"

◆

"There is a difference between a disaster and a calamity. This is a calamity."
— **Mike Espy**, U.S. Secretary of Agriculture

*I*n July, Sen. Tom Harkin rose on the floor of the United States Senate to appeal to his colleagues for disaster aid.

He noted that at one point in the summer of 1993, it rained for 50 out of 55 days in Iowa. He showed senators blown-up photographs of the devastation in Des Moines, small towns and the countryside. He produced a July 14 satellite picture of the state that showed massive amounts of moisture on the ground.

"It's as if we had Lake Erie in the heart of Iowa," Harkin said.

The story of the summer of 1993 was much more than the record flooding along the Mississippi River and the disaster that left Des Moines without water — although in a typical summer either of those events might have qualified as story of the year.

The story of 1993 was the record rainfall that drenched all of Iowa, leaving human misery and financial ruin in its wake.

"It's just water all over," said Iowa State University crop specialist Paul Kassel.

The flooding in Des Moines and along the Mississippi sometimes overpowered stories that in more normal times would have commanded the huge headlines and television bulletins.

There was the night in early July when the east and west forks of the Boyer River joined forces with severe weather to terrorize Denison. Nearly 8 inches of rain fell in a 7-hour period, causing flooding that closed the Farmland and IBP packing plants, idling 1,400 people.

Ames endured three floods from the Skunk River and Squaw Creek,

Derryl McLaren surveys his crop near Farragut.

BUZZ ORR

the first of which turned Hilton Coliseum into a murky swimming pool.

There were storms that forced families from their homes at Langworthy and Monticello and set the stage for emergencies later in Iowa City-Coralville, Columbus Junction, Wapello and Oakville, all towns held hostage for a time by the rampaging Iowa River.

The Iowa River caused significant damage to the University of Iowa campus, where graduation ceremonies for 1,500 summer graduates were cancelled. And only a massive sandbagging effort protected the city and university water-treatment plants from record torrents released from the Coralville Reservoir.

The Little Sioux River rose 4 feet in a few hours at Cherokee in northwest Iowa on July 18. Volunteers from as far as 60 miles away filled about 30,000 sandbags and helped to hold the water back.

In southwest Iowa, Hamburg and other towns on the Nishnabotna River and its tributaries spent the last week of July battling floodwaters caused by two weeks of downpours that dumped 20 inches of rain in the watershed.

There were dozens more stories like those all over Iowa: from Conesville, Colfax, Harlan, Redfield, Lacona, Missouri Valley, Perry, Kingston, Marshalltown, Manilla, Charles City and elsewhere.

Jerry DeMarce, Saylorville park manager, put his finger on Iowa's summer of 1993: "Normal is a word I don't understand anymore," he said. ∎

A view from the air of the Iowa State Center on the Iowa State University campus in Ames on July 9. As much as 14 feet of water filled Hilton Coliseum, right. University officials estimated campus damage at $7.7 million.

BOB NANDELL

Andy Long, left, a marketing official at the Iowa State Center, stood on flood watch behind the basketball scoreboard at Hilton Coliseum, where the water rose to 14 feet above floor level on July 9. After the water receded, Rob Netzel surveyed the damage. Silt remained after workers pumped 30 million gallons of floodwater from the arena.

BOB MODERSOHN

King's City Mobile Home Park in Ames was hard hit by flooding. Charlene Havens leans on the mailbox outside her home after learning that her insurance company would not cover losses. Elsewhere in the mobile home park, corn stalks on the hood of this car show how high floodwaters reached.

BOB MODERSOHN

**Floodwaters from the West Nishnabotna River between Sidney and Shenandoah
submerged these farm buildings along Highway 2.**

A sea of mud and water covered the lot of a grain elevator near the Denison business district July 9, after heavy rains hit western Iowa. Nitrogen tanks were swept into a pile by floodwaters from the Boyer River.

BOB NANDELL

The Iowa City-Coralville area was flooded in July and again in August. Here, Rebecca Gilpin and Victoria Gilpin help to load household items into a boat in Iowa City.

HARRY BAUMERT

**Bruce Gantenbein gets a chuckle out of a decorated mailbox
on an Iowa City street overrun with Iowa River water.**

HARRY BAUMERT

Jerry Schwartz uses a small tractor to scrape mud from the driveway of his accounting business in Denison.

BILL NEIBERGALL

Claud Hime drives his van near an Iowa City business that maintained a sense of humor about the flooding. The other side of the marquee read: "No fishing from parking lot."

HARRY BAUMERT

Jill Masonholder, 11, helps to build a dike at Columbus Junction on July 7.

HARRY BAUMERT

Two Rivers — One Catastrophe

*"You can plan or not plan and it doesn't make a hell of a lot of difference.
What makes a difference is how much it decides to rain."*

— **Mark Twain**, *Life on the Mississippi*

No one knows better than L.D. Mc-Mullen that Mark Twain was right.

McMullen is the director of the Des Moines Water Works, whose water-treatment plant sits hard by the banks of the Raccoon River. It's an area that floods frequently, so some years ago waterworks employees built a levee for the worst flooding imaginable. Then they added a foot or two for good measure.

In the early morning hours of July 11, the levee wasn't high enough.

The U.S. Geological Survey tweaked its computers and calculated that for about 13 hours on July 10, the Raccoon River bore down on Des Moines carrying more water than it might be expected to carry once in 500 years.

At the same time, the Des Moines River was taking aim at the heart of the city from another direction. Nick Melcher, chief of the Iowa district for the U.S. Geological Survey, said the computer was unable to determine whether the Des Moines achieved a 500-year flood. But, he said, "It appears to be in the range of a 500-year event."

Whatever the description, the two rivers delivered quite a pounding.

The metropolitan area sustained more than $700 million in property damage and in lost revenue.

Sherry Miller watches National Guard troops struggling to save a levee in her neighborhood.

DAVID PETERSON

"We've been bruised, but we're very healthy," said Michael Reagen of the Des Moines Chamber of Commerce.

The way people responded to the city's biggest catastrophe was summarized in the first few paragraphs of a July 19 article by *Des Moines Register* reporters Mary Ann Lickteig and Mary Challender:

Two rivers vs. 400,000 people.

If ever there was a test of the human spirit, this is it.

On one side are two tireless, dispassionate bodies of water. On the other, the exhausted residents of metro Des Moines.

The Raccoon and Des Moines rivers crashed through levees on July 10 and challenged us to the fight of our lives.

It's not one of those competitions where one person can make the miracle play, slam the ball out of the park and win one for Team Humanity. To beat the rivers, we've had to empty the stands, hand each spectator a bat and tell everyone to swing. Swing as if your life depended on it.

And the game goes on. When it's over, there will be no single Most Valuable Player. There will be thousands.

There already are. ■

A sandbagging volunteer works on the Raccoon River levee near 63rd Street and
Railroad Avenue on July 10, just before the levee gave way.

BOB NANDELL

The Raccoon River broke levees in West Des Moines, crossed Railroad Avenue and inundated the Valley Junction area July 10. The building at the lower left is located at about Ninth Street and Railroad Avenue.

BOB NANDELL

Their faces and poses painting a portrait of despair, Donna Hall and her son, Jeremy, look around their home in West Des Moines. Hall said she lost everything to the floodwaters.

DOUG WELLS

312

JUNE 17, 1990
HIGH WATER LINE

JULY 4, 1973

**Craig Laws, manager of Johnnie's Vet's Club, a popular West Des Moines restaurant known for its tenaci-
ty in weathering the area's floods, wades to the front door. The grimy line at the top marks the spot
where water receded after rising to the building's roof during the flood of '93.**

JYM WILSON

This view looks north on Fleur Drive toward downtown Des Moines. The street lights on the left form the eastern boundary of Water Works Park.

PAUL HISCOCKS

Workers take a rest from sandbagging on Fleur Drive on the south side of the Raccoon River on July 14.

DOUG WELLS

This is how the Raccoon River, the
Des Moines Water Works plant and
downtown Des Moines looked from the
air on July 11, Day One of the city's
worst natural disaster.

BOB NANDELL

Ann Marie and Ken McFadden of Clive take a break after help-ing to fill sandbags on the Fleur Drive bridge July 13.

JYM WILSON

National Guardsmen take cover behind a sandbag barrier as a helicopter takes off from the parking lot of the Farmland Insurance Companies. The parking lot was a staging area for the helicopters that transported sandbags to a levee around the Des Moines Water Works.

JYM WILSON

An unidentifed man rides a personal water craft on Des Moines Street, just east of the City Armory.

BOB NANDELL

Tom Daleske of Carlisle heads up deserted Seventh Street on his way to work at ACI Adhesive Compounds in Des Moines July 14.

JYM WILSON

Water pouring out of Saylorville Reservoir just north of Des Moines raised the river in downtown Des Moines to its highest level since the dam was built in 1965. On July 11, the day Des Moines lost its water, sightseers lined the Court Avenue Bridge. This tree limb was lodged against the same bridge later in the week.

JYM WILSON
BOB NANDELL

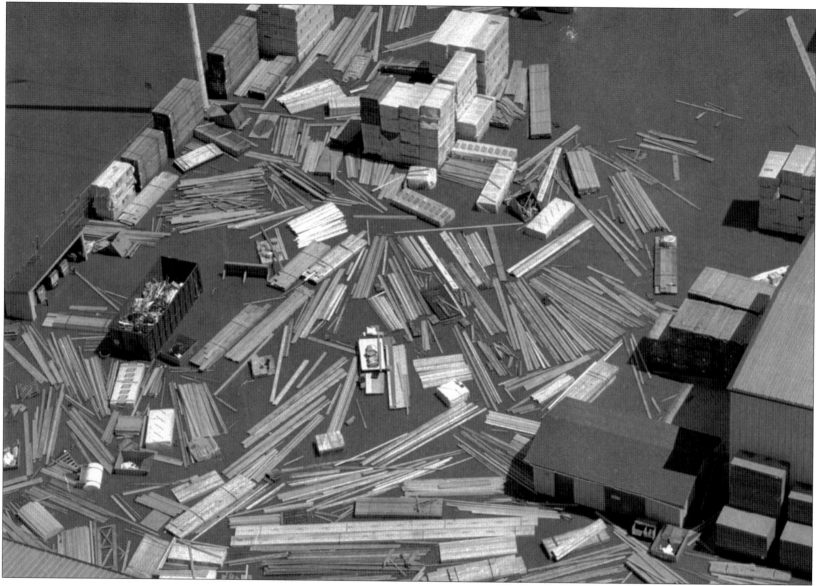

Lumber floats in a flooded yard south of Court Avenue near downtown Des Moines. The flooding rivers hit several downtown businesses and industrial parks especially hard.

BOB NANDELL

Court Avenue flooding put several restaurants out of business temporarily. Johnny's Hall of Fame Lounge displayed this help-wanted sign.

BOB NANDELL

It helped to have a sense of humor. When water flooded the Iowa Cubs' clubhouse and ruined some equipment, team physician Richard Evans bought some fish, planted them in pitcher Turk Wendell's waterlogged glove and left the glove in Wendell's locker.

JEFFREY Z. CARNEY

The lack of water caused a number of problems. Several breweries solved one of them by providing water in beer cans. Restaurants had to wait until July 22 to make fountain drinks.

BOB NANDELL

Des Moines residents wait in line at one of the city's 92 temporary water distribution sites, this one in a Hy-Vee store parking lot at 2700 Ingersoll Ave.

DOUG WELLS

Volunteer Irvin Polson of Des Moines directs traffic to the water distribution center at Anderson Erickson Dairy on East University Avenue in Des Moines.

DAVID PETERSON

Bill Smith, 67, of Des Moines, catches rain pouring off his garage roof. Many residents used the abundant rainwater for flushing toilets.

BOB MODERSOHN

Restaurants were allowed to reopen before water service was restored, but they had to provide sanitary facilities. This is how a Des Moines Hardee's restaurant provided hand-washing supplies for customers.

DOUG WELLS

Jane Graves of Des Moines pushes 15-month-old Crystal and pulls empty water jugs on her way to the store.

DAVID PETERSON

Among the busiest people in town after the flooding were employees of the Des Moines Water Works. Workers had to clean mud and silt from buildings and fix the giant pumps that move water through 850 miles of pipes. Donald Jones, left, a worker at 3E Electrical Engineering Co., paints coils in one of the pump motors that was removed for cleaning.

GARY FANDEL
BOB NANDELL

When the water came back in Des Moines, Glen Goehme Jr., a waterworks employee, helped to bleed air from the water system at a fire hydrant near East Aurora and Colfax avenues.

BOB MODERSOHN

L.D. McMullen, director of the Des Moines Water Works, celebrates the return of water with his children, Lisa, 18, and Lane, 15. McMullen became one of the city's most recognizable faces.

TERESA HURTEAU

John and Bobby, 7-year-old twin sons of Ann and David Ketch of Des Moines, took a bath shortly after water was restored to homes on July 22.

GARY FANDEL

Picking Up the Pieces

◆

"We've got to pick up the pieces and go on. That's what Americans do, and that's what we're going to have to do."

— **President Bill Clinton**, in Des Moines, July 14, 1993

Rebuilding flooded Iowa would be a tall order.

Even the very early damage assessments were eye-popping: Metropolitan Des Moines — $716 million; Lee County — $44 million; Crawford County — $32 million; Story County — $17 million, including $7.7 million at Iowa State University; Johnson County — $4.5 million at the University of Iowa alone.

In Polk County, one in seven businesses applied for disaster assistance from the Federal Emergency Management Agency.

All along rivers and streams, thousands of acres of rich farmland and countless farm buildings sat soaking. Iowa Agriculture Secretary Dale Cochran estimated $1 billion in damage to Iowa crops drowned by high water or stunted from cool, wet weather.

Other damage could not be measured so easily with dollar signs.

Sixty Ottumwa families from the area known as Rabbit Run were chased from their homes by the Des Moines River on July 5. Late in the summer, when most Iowans were back in their homes and cleaning up, Sheila and Dick Damm and their neighbors were still waiting. Stubborn floodwaters refused to recede and the Ottumwans faced the prospect of being homeless for months.

Sheila Damm likened the flood, and all the changes it brought, to death. The emotional toll has been like the loss of a loved one, she said.

Though smudged, this teddy bear was recovered.

BOB MODERSOHN

Mental health experts also worried about long-term emotional problems created by the stress of coping with floods, including "dripping-faucet stress": Each drop may not be annoying, but collectively they are enormously disturbing. For Iowans, the "dripping" included a lack of sunshine, detours, potholes, working without water and air conditioning, government bureaucracy and a lack of cash — all resulting in a "heightened vulnerability to personal problems," said psychiatrist Loren Olson.

By late summer, Iowans appeared to be heeding President Clinton's advice. They were picking up the pieces.

Some were spending down their savings accounts. Some were applying for federal grants. Still others were counting on the goodwill of dozens of volunteers who came to Iowa from every corner of America to do what they could to help.

And some were drawing valuable lessons from the experience.

Volunteer Susan VanRees, 20, paused one day while shoveling smelly sludge from a basement in the Valley Garden neighborhood near the Des Moines Water Works and talked about what she had learned.

"It makes you thankful for what you have," she said. "It makes you realize the power of the river, the power of God — that we're not in control of things." ■

What goes up must come down, eventually. These photographs were taken at a softball complex along Interstate Highways 35-80 just north of Des Moines, as water receded over a two-week period.

BOB MODERSOHN

Kevin Swecker, a volunteer from St. Paul, Minn., heaves a waterlogged table onto a pile of other damaged household goods from a house on West 60th Street in Des Moines. A group of about 500 volunteers came from the Twin Cities to help.

DAVID PETERSON

Standing on their deck in the Morningstar Drive area of Des Moines, Jack and Donna Karpan view the damage done to their 35-acre farm, which was entirely covered by water. "I don't want to come back. It makes you sick," Donna Karpan said. The deck is braced by a tractor to keep it from floating away.

PAUL HISCOCKS

Despair written all over his face, Ernie Harms of the St. George Doll Co. looks at the flood disaster that destroyed his business at Clark and Ohio streets in Des Moines. Harms holds three doll heads he managed to pluck from the debris. Other doll heads and parts, covered with dirt and oil, were piled into a box at the plant.

BOB NANDELL

Flooding brought celebrities and national media figures to Iowa. ABC News anchor Peter Jennings, above, anchored the nightly news from Des Moines on July 14, as did CBS's Dan Rather and NBC's Tom Brokaw. Iowa native Andy Williams returned to help distribute water in Des Moines one morning. And, the Rev. Jesse Jackson made several visits to Iowa.

DOUG WELLS
JEFFREY Z. CARNEY
TERESA HURTEAU

Even the mayor got involved with flood
cleanup. Des Moines Mayor John "Pat"
Dorrian helps to clear debris from his
office at the Plumbers and Steamfitters
Local 33 office on Bell Avenue.

When Des Moines lost its water, help arrived from all over.
This package of disposable diapers, donated by people in Denver, bore messages for its Iowa recipients.

DOUG WELLS

Des Moines Postmaster Norm Griese,
left, and District Manager Tom Johnson sort through some of the 10,000
letters that were caught in the flood at
the post office's Morgan Street Annex.
The mail was separated and dried —
and, in the case of the most damaged
letters, sponged off and ironed.

DOUG WELLS

Waterless residents wait patiently outside a laundromat in Altoona for their turn to use the busy and scarce washing machines.

DOUG WELLS

Necessity often breeds stoicism as well
as invention. Joshua Brown, 8, washed
his hair and his mother, Judy Brown,
rinsed it with a pan of rainwater during
a downpour July 13.

BOB MODERSOHN

Not a moment too soon, Teledyne Water Pik's shower truck arrived in Des Moines on July 16. The "Original Shower Massage Traveling Showers," with 14 stalls and 14 low waterflow shower heads, was set up at the Southtown Swimming Pool. Paulette Stamper, foreground, and Rosalie Wagner smile as they come out.

BOB MODERSOHN

Roxanne Rogers looks up at a helicopter hovering overhead. Rogers was helping to clean the Des Moines home of her sister, Joanne Wright.

TERESA HURTEAU

WHY IOWA WAS SO WET

THE HEAVY RAINS in Iowa and the rest of the Midwest in the summer of 1993 were largely due to a lingering jet stream. The stream, described as "a river of air" by one forecaster, flows at an altitude of 25,000-35,000 feet. It travels at 30-50 mph but has been known to reach nearly 100 mph. Here's an explanation of the phenomenon that put Iowa under water.

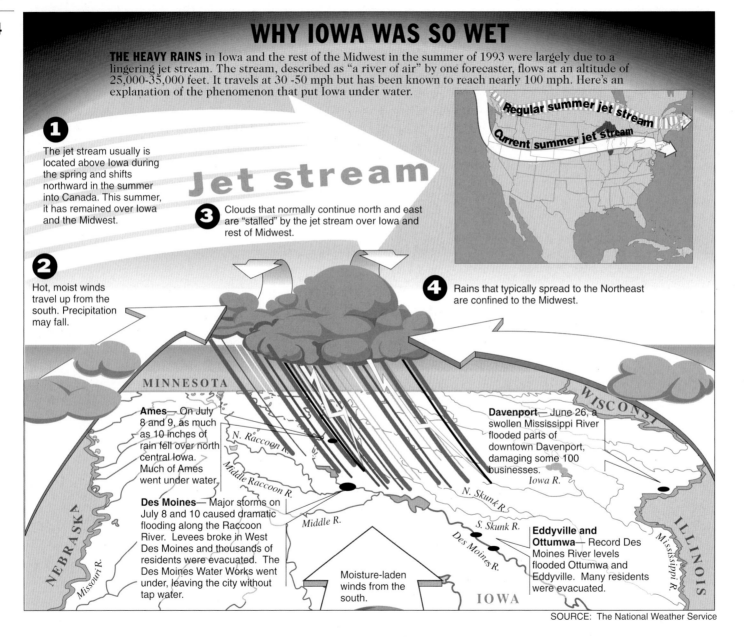

Regular summer jet stream

Current summer jet stream

Jet stream

1 The jet stream usually is located above Iowa during the spring and shifts northward in the summer into Canada. This summer, it has remained over Iowa and the Midwest.

3 Clouds that normally continue north and east are "stalled" by the jet stream over Iowa and rest of Midwest.

2 Hot, moist winds travel up from the south. Precipitation may fall.

4 Rains that typically spread to the Northeast are confined to the Midwest.

MINNESOTA

WISCONSIN

Ames— On July 8 and 9, as much as 10 inches of rain fell over north central Iowa. Much of Ames went under water.

N. Raccoon R.

Middle Raccoon R.

Davenport— June 26, a swollen Mississippi River flooded parts of downtown Davenport, damaging some 100 businesses.

Iowa R.

N. Skunk R.

Des Moines— Major storms on July 8 and 10 caused dramatic flooding along the Raccoon River. Levees broke in West Des Moines and thousands of residents were evacuated. The Des Moines Water Works went under, leaving the city without tap water.

Middle R.

S. Skunk R.

Des Moines R.

Eddyville and Ottumwa— Record Des Moines River levels flooded Ottumwa and Eddyville. Many residents were evacuated.

NEBRASKA

Missouri R.

Moisture-laden winds from the south.

IOWA

ILLINOIS

Mississippi R.

SOURCE: The National Weather Service

In Iowa, We Endure

Reprinted in part from The Des Moines Register,
July 13, 1993.

We don't know who they are, but they are always there, these anonymous links in the human chain.

It's the stranger standing next to you in the sandbag line. The cook who volunteers to help at the American Red Cross shelter. The Urbandale minister who cancels his church service and tells the congregation to go help somebody. The two men who show up in your neighborhood with a tanker truck full of safe water.

For the past three days, the Des Moines area has witnessed more random acts of kindness than can ever be documented fully. Can there exist a minister who hasn't fashioned a sermon around the notion of finding something good in a bad situation? Can there be a more whiskered cliche?

Doesn't make it any less true.

"I met this guy, a Nashville singer, who was performing somewhere downtown," says Tom Vlassis, a member of the Des Moines City Council. "He's down there at the library sandbagging with us at 4 a.m. Sunday morning. I couldn't believe it."

Like everyone else in Des Moines, residents on 45th Street between Kingman Boulevard and University Avenue had no safe water to drink. Then Kenny and Wes

A t-shirt sums up Iowa's response.

JEFFREY Z. CARNEY

Sweedler arrived.

The Sweedlers, father and son from Williams, own Alpine Liquid Plant Food. They drained a 1,600-gallon tanker truck, sanitized it twice, filled it with chlorinated water and delivered it to the people along 45th Street, where Kenny Sweedler's brother-in-law lives.

Wes Sweedler has planted two crops this year. Both have flooded.

"We're not as bad off as you are down here," he says. "You can always find somebody worse off than you."

We expect these gestures in rural Iowa. A farmer falls ill; his neighbors harvest the crops. A child needs an operation; they pass the hat at a Little League game. The man down the street dies; the entire neighborhood brings food for the survivors.

But this is Des Moines, the big city, home of mean headlines and cruel deeds.

It is also the home of Randy Bauer.

Bauer, a budget analyst for the Iowa Legislature, had the day off, so he spent Monday filling sandbags, one day after he returned home from his honeymoon. "I'm just doing what I can to help out," he says.

During their daily disaster briefings, Des Moines officials marvel at the cooperation shown, from government agencies that are supposed to help to citizens who feel it is their duty.

When the floods struck, Des Moines Mayor John "Pat" Dorrian says his telephone calls shifted from complaints about barking dogs and illegally parked cars to just one question: What can I do to help?

"I was just overwhelmed," he says.

Dorrian calls it part of the Midwestern ethic. There are no tent cities or soup lines here, he said. Most of the 5,000 people evacuated from their homes have found shelter with friends, neighbors and loved ones.

But Iowans hold no copyright on the Golden Rule. Jean Larsen, a registered nurse at Iowa Lutheran Hospital, volunteered to help in Homestead, Fla., after the hurricane hit. She said tragic situations bring out the best in people.

On Monday, Larsen was volunteering again, this time at the American Red Cross shelter in West Des Moines. She describes how strangers walk in with supplies of shampoo, towels and clothes — "No name, no number, just, 'Here's a bag,' " she says.

Why do they do it? Why does Larsen do it?

" 'Cause you're supposed to," she says.

If there is a symbol of community spirit, it is the sandbag line. Every time a call for help goes out, it seems 500 people show up.

A bag is filled and moves down the line, from the black hand to the white hand to the young hand to the old hand, from the hand of the sorority sister to the skinhead, from the lawyer to the laid-off factory worker, from the street bum to the street sweeper.

They pile the bags until the bags become a wall. From one hand to the next, they fight water the way their ancestors once fought fires.

Sometimes the wall crumbles, as it did Saturday night in Valley Junction in West Des Moines. Sometimes the wall holds, as it did Sunday at the water treatment plant in West Des Moines. It doesn't matter. The people keep coming back.

Lloyd Austin watched sandbaggers work Monday to protect his Austin Trailer Leasing building on 13th Street in West Des Moines.

"That did my heart good, to see all the people helping out — muddy clear to their ears," says Austin, 75. "They really seemed to enjoy doing some good."

Then Austin said something probably more profound than he intended: "I don't know them, but I know them."

You know Vetty Lenzley, 60, who worked on the sandbag line even though his own basement was flooded. "I gotta help somewhere," he says.

You know Beth Hanna, the food service director for the West Des Moines school district, who volunteered to coordinate the efforts of the Red Cross and Salvation Army to feed refugees. She worked all weekend, but shrugged off her contribution.

You know Rosa Ramsey, 70, a Des Moines woman who calls herself Santa Claus. Although she lives on a fixed income, Ramsey collects toys all year and distributes them every Christmas to poor children. When her home was flooded and she was forced to leave, Ramsey insisted that the toys be taken out first.

You know these people because they represent the best and only weapon we truly hold against the inevitable tragedies and travails.

Robert Hullihan, the late *Des Moines Register* reporter, wrote a tribute to the cartoonist Frank Miller that referred to Miller's life philosophy:

"He knew its truths, its lies, its shabby propositions, its rare moments of grace and triumph and fun, and he knew that, most of the time, we lose. But he also knew that, in Iowa, most of the time, we also endure."

The rain may return. The rivers may grow. The damage may worsen. But the Vetty Lenzleys, Beth Hannas and Rosa Ramseys will still be here.

The fight's not over.
But we've won.

—Ken Fuson

Summary of Events from the Flood of 1993

◆

March 27: Runoff from snow melt causes rivers to rise, but no major flooding is predicted.

March 31: Record flood levels widespread in north Iowa. New Hartford is cut off.

April 1: Record flooding persists. Gov. Terry Branstad declares Black Hawk, Butler, Floyd, Humboldt, Kossuth, Mitchell, Tama and Wright counties disaster areas.

April 4: *Des Moines Register* headline: 'Worst is over' in flooded north. In Tama, 107 families evacuated.

April 8: West Des Moines, Des Moines and Army Corps of Engineers announce construction of 4-mile levee, to begin in fall 1993, to protect 900 acres of Raccoon River and Walnut Creek floodplain.

April 20: Snow returns, as do flood fears. New Hartford has flooding again.

May 2: President Clinton declares Benton, Buchanan, Muscatine and Webster federal disaster areas, joining Black Hawk, Butler, Linn and Tama counties.

May 7: Saylorville bike trail submerged. Barges back up on Mississippi River.

May 26: Main swim area of Saylorville floods as Memorial Day weekend approaches.

May 28: *Register* headline: "Believe it or not, forecasters see a drought."

June 15: Saylorville down to one boat ramp.

June 19: Storms rage again over water-logged state, destroying buildings, washing out bridges and producing spot flooding. April Dedrick, 22, and Shayna Lee Stewart, 19, of Vinton, die when their car plunges into 10-foot deep ravine caused by flash flooding.

June 20: The Des Moines River at Stratford

7 feet above flood stage.

June 25: Locks close on Mississippi. Barges backed up.

June 28: Iowa National Guard fills sandbags as flooding hits Davenport. John O'Donnell Stadium under water. Branstad adds 15 counties to disaster list.

June 29: Heavy rains douse north. Tornadoes spotted from Altoona to Fort Dodge. Blinding rain and winds up to 60 mph. D.M. temperatures drop 15 degrees in one hour.

June 30: Mississippi almost 6 feet above flood stage. Davenport evacuates hundreds. Flash flood warnings in southern two-thirds of state. Additional National Guard troops sent to Quad Cities. Agriculture Secretary Mike Espy tours northeast Iowa. Des Moines County residents sandbag and prepare to evacuate. Hurricane-force winds in Waterloo.

July 1: Clinton pledges farm relief; plans to visit Iowa. Hundreds abandon homes. Record river level at Burlington. The past eight months set record as "wettest ever — by a long way," says state climatologist Harry Hillaker.

July 2: Mississippi swells at Davenport. National Guard shores up levees. Record level at Saylorville. Coast Guard orders pleasure boats off Mississippi. Corps discharging enormous amounts of water in Iowa's interior. Saylorville increases outflow enough to raise river 3 feet. Coralville Reservoir 38 feet higher than normal.

July 3: Flood damage estimated at $1 billion. More highways close.

July 4: Clinton visits Quad Cities area. Mississippi crests at 7 feet above flood stage,

second-highest in 155 years.

July 5: Rain continues. Levee washes out in Eddyville. Coralville Reservoir over spillway for first time in 35-year history. Campers evacuated from Monticello park. Record river levels at Burlington and Keokuk. Water main wiped out in Lacona.

July 6: Oakville evacuated. Red Cross sets up shelters. Lower Des Moines River towns evacuated. Parts of Iowa City and Coralville paralyzed. Two miles of I-80 near Iowa City closed. Drinking water threatened in several communities.

July 7: Levees fail along Iowa River. In Louisa County, 800 flee. Levee breached at Columbus Junction. Vernon Neiderhiser, 70, of Ely, drowns when his car plunges into flood waters. National Guard call-ups now at 650, on way to 4,200.

July 8: Wild night in central Iowa — tornado sightings; up to 7.5 inches of rain in Manilla; another 7.83 inches in Jefferson; 2,500 families evacuated. Rainfall in Iowa for 37 of the last 40 days. Coralville Reservoir backs into nearby Lake Macbride.

July 9: Iowa River sets record crest at Marshalltown. Record flooding predicted for Valley Junction area of W.D.M. I-35 closed between Ames and D.M. Portions of Ames and Iowa State University severely flooded. Hilton Coliseum submerged under 14 feet of water. Corps warns that Saylorville, Coralville and Red Rock reservoirs are at capacity. Mississippi crests 7 feet above flood stage at Davenport.

July 10: Effort to protect Valley Junction fails, forcing evacuation of 5,000 people. Final day of Ruan Greater Des Moines

Grand Prix cancelled. Raccoon River in W.D.M. rises a foot an hour. Donald Sealine, 64, and his wife, Bernadine, 67, of rural Dexter, drowned when their livestock truck plunged into the flooded Nishnabotna River near Carson. State Patrol cautions motorists to stay out of Iowa.

July 11: Estimated 250,000 residents of Des Moines and surrounding communities without water after Water Works is flooded. Estimated 35,000 to 40,000 Midwest Power customers without electricity. States of emergency declared in D.M. and W.D.M. Truckloads of safe water pour into city. Evacuations continue. Safe water not expected for one month.

July 12: Skunk River crests at Colfax, damaging 50 homes. Eddyville gives up 8-day fight against the river.

July 13: Entire state declared disaster area; power restored in much of Des Moines. I-380 between Iowa City and Cedar Rapids is closed by Coralville Reservoir backup. Cedar Rapids sewer system back on line after brief shutdown.

July 14: Clinton spends five hours in D.M., touring city by helicopter, then meeting with flood victims at water-distribution site.

July 15: D.M. Mayor Dorrian orders all non-essential businesses closed until water restored. Section of I-80 east of D.M. closed by water damage, forcing motorists to take 80-mile detour.

July 16: Iowa National Guard Spc. Steven West of Ogden electrocuted while on duty in D.M.

July 17: Ames hit by flooding again. National Guard troops rebuild crumbling levee in southeast D.M. While inspecting the levee, Mayor Dorrian and Councilman Archie Brooks almost come to blows. Hardin County gets 5 inches of rain.

July 18: Cherokee flooded by Little Sioux River. Anamosa and Toledo get 5 inches of rain. D.M. begins refilling water system.

July 19: The University of Iowa cancels summer graduation ceremonies. Ross Perot makes a quick stop in D.M. Two Denison packing plants knocked out by floods in early July reopen, as does a Mississippi River bridge at Keokuk. First reports of water "cheating" in D.M.

July 20: Iowa City sandbags its water treatment plant as Iowa River rises. D.M. Councilman Brooks, who also manages 36-story Ruan Center, cuts power to the city police and fire antennae, limiting communications for hours. Brooks' action came after waterworks employee mistakenly cut off water to Ruan building.

July 21: D.M. water system is filled.

July 22: D.M. residents turn on taps for first time in 12 days, although water not yet safe for drinking.

July 23: Fremont County gets 6 inches of rain. Missouri and Nishnabotna rivers rage.

July 24: Nishnabotna overruns levee at Hamburg. Flooding knocks out water plant at St. Joseph, Mo.

July 25: Iowa flooding claims seventh life. Kenneth Tille, 43, of Knoxville dies when his car is swept into Des Moines River at closed bridge. Fierce gusts of wind — sufficient to push around an airplane weighing 110,000 pounds — hit D.M. airport.

July 26: Hamburg reports 20 inches of rain in 2 ½ weeks. Most D.M. businesses return. Jet stream finally shifts, promising end to constant rain.

July 27: Mississippi River falls below flood stage at Dubuque.

July 28: Iowa transportation officials tally damage: 40 bridges; 60 highways. Contractors put road damage at $500 million.

July 29: Iowa television stations, joined by nationwide network, produce flood telethon.

July 30: Des Moines water declared safe to drink.

August 16: The Cedar River swamps Charles City and creates problems in Nashua, Plainfield, Waverly and Janesville. The South Skunk River and Squaw Creek flood Ames for third time.

August 17: Tama flooded a fourth time; Chelsea for the fifth time. A levee break on the Turkey River floods Elgin. Iowa River comes within inches of breaking 38-day-old flood record at Marshalltown.

August 22: Mississippi River open for barge traffic for the first time since June 25.

August 29: More than 5 inches of rain in 24 hours causes widespread flooding and sewer back-ups in Des Moines and suburbs. Raccoon River crests at 19.7 feet at Fleur Drive, fourth highest ever, but below 26.7-foot record of July 11.

BILL NEIBERGALL

A s this book went to press in late August, rain and flooding continued to threaten Iowa.

Officials at the U.S. Army Corps of Engineers and researchers at Iowa State University and the University of Iowa said huge rains since spring had brought the water table to within inches of the surface of the ground.

They said Iowa and much of the rest of the Midwest remained vulnerable to flooding through the spring of 1994. ■